This book
belongs to:

My thanks to editor Kristen McCurry. Thanks also to my bird word listeners: Jeff Sayre, Andrea Rogers, Barb Crighton, Barb and Joe Linney, and Maureen Shindeldecker. Special thanks to Kenn Kaufman; his book Lives of North American Birds *should be in every family's home library to help answer the questions spawned by this book.* —A.P.S.

For Elizabeth, my smart, nature-loving niece
—A. P. S.

For my Grandma and Grandpa Locke,
whose never-ending patience was tested every time I went fishing
and searching for the great blue heron of the Walnut River
—G.L.

The illustrations were created using watercolor, colored pencil, airbrush, and Adobe Photoshop
The text and display type were set in DaddyO Hip and Sniplash
Composed in the United States of America
Art directed and designed by Lois A. Rainwater
Edited by Kristen McCurry

Text © 2007 by April Pulley Sayre
Illustrations © 2007 by Gary Locke

NorthWord
Books for Young Readers
11571 K-Tel Drive
Minnetonka, MN 55343
www.tnkidsbooks.com

Library of Congress Cataloging-in-Publication Data

Sayre, April Pulley.
Bird, bird, bird : a chirping chant / by April Pulley Sayre ; illustrated by Gary Locke.
p. cm.
ISBN 978-1-55971-978-0 (hc)
1. Birds--North America--Juvenile literature. 2. Birds--North America--Nomenclature (Popular)--Juvenile literature. I. Locke, Gary, ill. II. Title.

QL681.S385 2007
598--dc22   2007000140

Printed in Singapore
10 9 8 7 6 5 4 3 2 1

BiRD, BiRD, BiRD!

(A Chirping Chant)

by
April Pulley Sayre

illustrated by
Gary Locke

NorthWord
Minnetonka, Minnesota

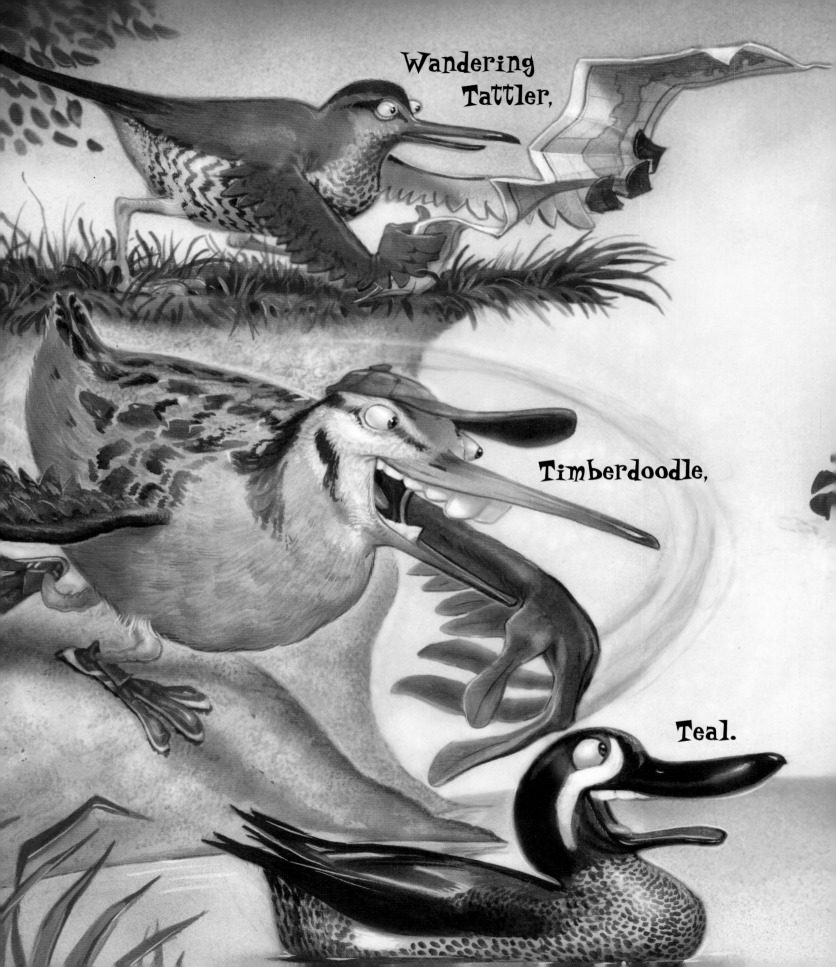

Wandering Tattler,

Timberdoodle,

Teal.

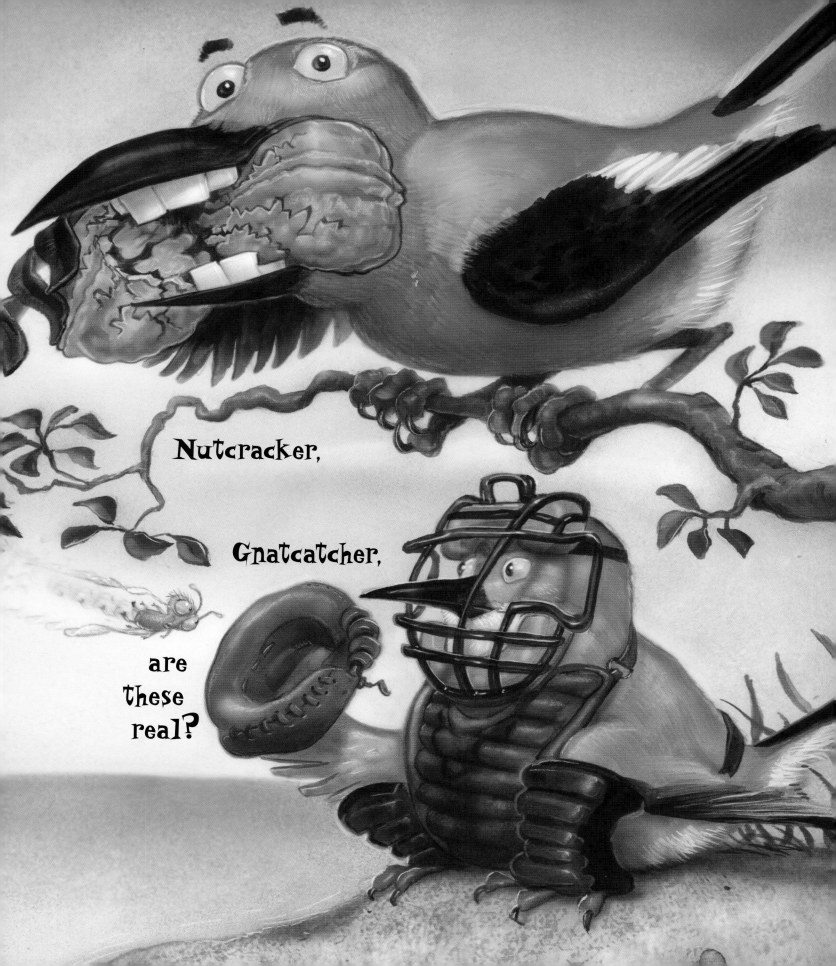

Yellow-bellied Sapsucker,

picture that!

Bufflehead,

Shoveler,

both are fowl.

Bald Eagle,

Bobolink,

Burrowing Owl.

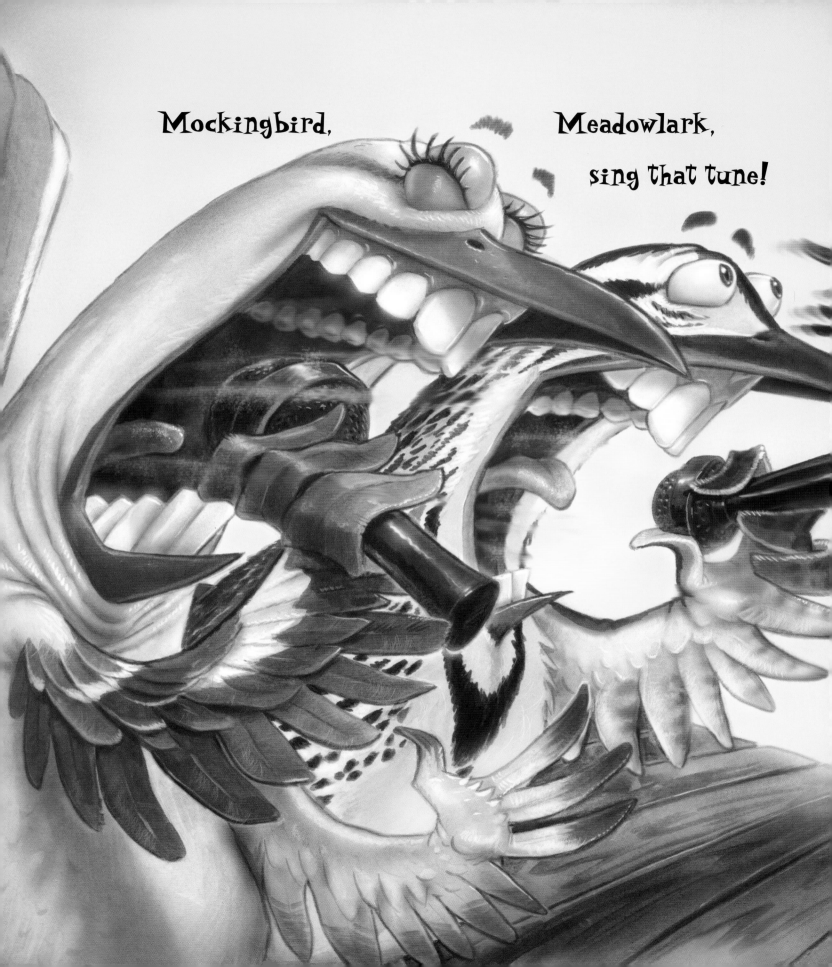

Mockingbird,

Meadowlark,

sing that tune!

Towhee,

Tanager,

Loon,
Loon,
Loon!

Kingbird,

Kingfisher,

Kite.

Kinglet,

Frigatebird,
my word,
what a
sight!

Grackle,

Grosbeak,

Sharp-shinned Hawk.

Whooping
Crane,

Laughing Gull,

Auk,
Auk,
Auk!

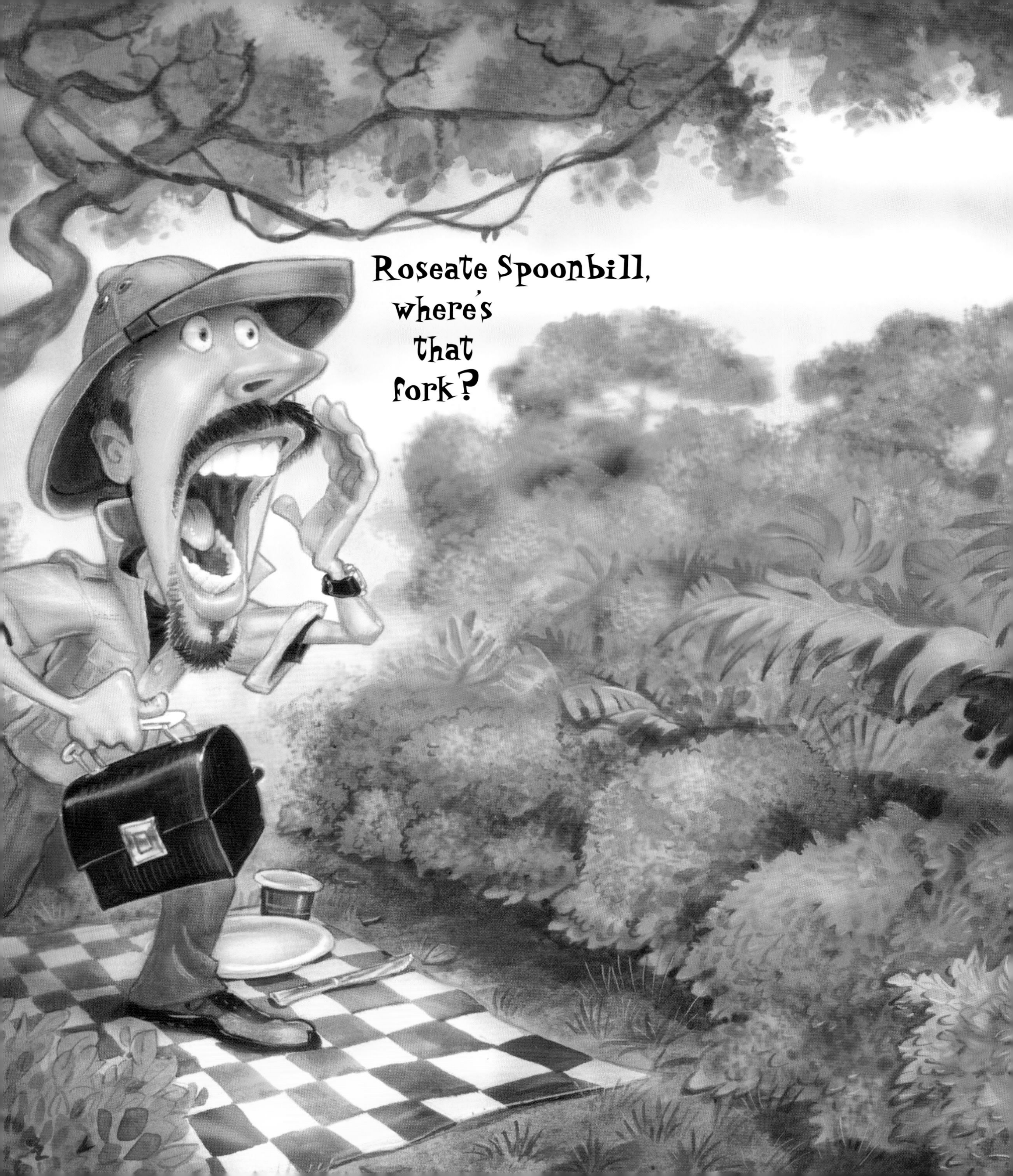

Roseate Spoonbill,
where's
that
fork?

Scissor-tailed Flycatcher,

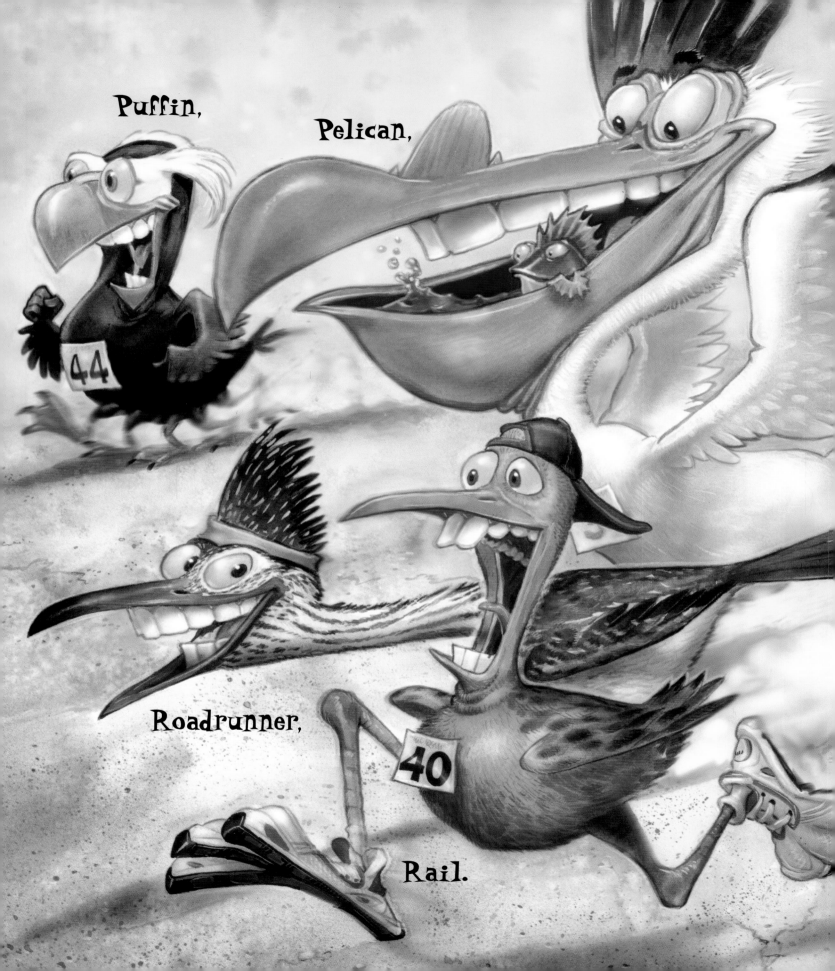

Puffin,

Pelican,

Roadrunner,

Rail.

Worm-eating Warbler,

Woodpecker,

Wigeon.

Snow Goose,

Sage Grouse,

great display!

Bluebird, Blackbird,

Bobwhite, Brant.

White-winged Dove.

Birds, Birds,
Birds,
that's what
I love!

Hooray for American Birds!

America has a variety of birds, from California condors to worm-eating warblers. Around 900 bird species inhabit North America north of the border with Mexico. Some American birds migrate, making regular yearly journeys. They may spend most of the year in Mexico, Central America, or South America. So these "American" birds are truly international treasures.

Wandering Tattler

These gray shorebirds hunt for insects, worms, and crabs along the rocky coasts of Alaska, Canada, and California. They do wander, flying all the way to Hawaii!

Timberdoodle

Timberdoodles, also known as American woodcocks, use their long bills to probe for earthworms. On spring evenings listen for their calls and whirring wings as they spiral skyward in courtship displays.

Teal

The blue-winged teal is a small, fast-flying duck that eats mainly seeds but also snails and insects. Most blue-winged teal spend the winter in Mexico, Central America, and South America.

Nutcracker

A Clark's nutcracker uses its bill to chisel into pinecones and extract seeds. It stashes some seeds in soil then eats them in winter. Some seeds, left behind in the soil, grow into new trees.

Gnatcatcher

The blue-gray gnatcatcher is a tiny, active insect-eater with a high-pitched call. It wraps its nest with spider webs and camouflages it with lichen.

Yellow-bellied Sapsucker

These colorful woodpeckers tap holes in trees and lick the sweet sap that oozes out.

Chachalaca

Plain chachalaca are named for their loud cha-cha-lac calls. They walk the ground and climb trees to find their food: berries, seeds, buds, and leaves.

Chickadee

Like many birds, black-capped chickadees need partly rotten trees and dead branches as sites for their nests.

Chat

The yellow-breasted chat is North America's largest warbler. Loudly whistling and chirping, it is more often heard than seen.

Bufflehead

Buffleheads are the smallest ducks in North America.

Shoveler

Northern shovelers use their wide bills to sift through water for seeds, small insects, and fish. Shovelers, like buffleheads, are waterfowl— web-footed swimming birds such as ducks, geese, and swans.

Bald Eagle

Bald eagles hunt mostly fish, but also ducks and small animals. They also steal food from other predators.

Bobolink

Bobolinks are small grassland birds. Their song, a bubbly "bob-o-link," sounds like the R2-D2 droid in *Star Wars*.

Burrowing Owl

Burrowing owls dig a burrow as long as 10 feet. Or, they may move into a burrow left by a prairie dog or armadillo.

Mockingbird

Northern mockingbirds are famous for their ability to imitate other birds' calls and even car alarms.

Meadowlark

The beautiful, bubbling call of the eastern meadowlark means spring to many people. These birds often sing from fence posts.

Towhee

Eastern towhees eat berries and scratch among fallen leaves to find insects and seeds. Their song sounds like "Drink your tea!"

Tanager

Male scarlet tanagers are bright scarlet during breeding season. But after breeding season, they molt those feathers and grow olive-yellow feathers.

Loon

Famous for their yodeling calls, common loons eat fish and nest on the banks of ponds and lakes.

Kingbird

Western kingbirds often perch on fence posts. These flycatchers snatch grasshoppers, beetles, wasps, and other insects out of the air.

Kingfisher

Belted kingfishers dive into streams and ponds to catch small fish. To nest, they dig tunnels 3 to 6 feet long into sandy stream banks.

Kinglet

Golden-crowned kinglets are tiny birds with a golden stripe of feathers on their heads. They nest in conifers, which are trees that have cones.

Kite

Swallow-tailed kites swoop and glide, catching insects midair, over Florida and nearby southeastern states.

Frigatebird

During courtship, the male frigatebird inflates its bright red throat patch.

Grackle

Common grackles may look dark black in the shade. But in the right light, you can see their beautiful blue-purple sheen.

Grosbeak

Rose-breasted grosbeaks get their name from the word "gros" which means big. Their big beaks help them crack the seeds they eat.

Sharp-shinned Hawk

These small hawks can fly quickly through forests, dodging tree trunks as they hunt for smaller birds.

Whooping Crane

These rare cranes really do have a "whooping" call. Conservationists are breeding them to bring them back from the brink of extinction.

Laughing Gull

Like many gull species, laughing gulls do not grow in their darker, adult feathers until they are several years old. Laughing gulls' calls do sound a little bit like people laughing.

Auk

Now extinct, great auks were good swimmers but could not fly. So when sailors came ashore they could easily catch and kill the nesting auks. The last ones died in the 1800s. The great auk's living relatives are the smaller murrelets, guillemots, and auklets.

Roseate Spoonbill

Wading in lagoons, marshes, and mangroves, spoonbills sweep their bills from side to side, feeling for small fish, shrimp, insects, and plants.

More American Birds!

Scissor-tailed Flycatcher

These long-tailed birds perch on wires in open country in Texas and nearby states.

Stint

The red-necked stint and little stint are sandpipers more commonly seen in Europe and Asia than the U.S. But they sometimes show up in Alaska.

Stilt

Black-necked stilts have red, narrow, stilt-like legs. Stilts feed on insects, snails, crayfish, and other small creatures in mudflats.

Stork

With its 5-foot wingspan, a wood stork is an impressive sight. Wood storks hunt for fish, crayfish, and frogs.

Puffin

Tufted puffins dive, swim, and hunt fish in the Pacific Ocean. The male and female both help dig a deep nesting burrow into a sea cliff.

Pelican

American white pelicans float on the water and scoop up fish. They sometimes work in groups, herding fish toward one another.

Roadrunner

Greater roadrunners can fly, but mostly they run—at speeds of 15 miles per hour or more. Roadrunners hunt insects, tarantulas, centipedes, and lizards.

Rail

Virginia rails live in marshes and hunt insects, snails, and crayfish.

Barn Swallow

Barn swallows nest inside barns and under bridges. They swoop out and feed on insects.

Tree Swallow

Tree swallows nest in holes in trees but also make use of bluebird houses. Often people build two houses, side-by-side. Bluebirds nest in one, and swallows in the other.

Quail

The California quail is a seed-eating, ground-walking bird that lives in small flocks called coveys.

Worm-eating Warbler

Worm-eating warblers search wooded hillsides for caterpillars, beetles, and other insects. Worm-eating warblers nest on the ground.

Woodpecker

Pileated woodpeckers peck on wood to reach the grubs underneath the bark. Woodpeckers carve out nest holes in trees. Their old nesting holes become homes for owls, wood ducks, and raccoons.

Wigeon

The American wigeon is a duck that eats plants in fields, marshes, lakes, and large ponds.

Piping Plover

Areas of Atlantic and Great Lakes beaches are sometimes closed for a few weeks to allow this endangered bird to raise its chicks in peace.

Poorwill

The common poorwill's call sounds like a soft, mournful "poor-will." At night these birds fly out and grab moths and other insects from the air.

Pintail

Northern pintails are named for their long, thin tails. Pintails live from Mexico to Alaska, and some live in Asia as well.

Pigeon

The common pigeon, also called "rock dove," originally lived in Europe, Asia, and Africa, but now lives wild in the U.S. Male and female pigeons feed their babies "pigeon milk," a milky fluid that drips from the parent's mouth.

Snow Goose

Snow geese eat plants, including grain leftover in farm fields. The population has increased significantly in the last 100 years.

Sage Grouse

Sage grouse eat sagebrush leaves. Each year sage grouse gather in the same place. The males puff up and perform a dramatic strutting dance to attract females.

California Condor

California condors have a wingspan of more than 9 feet. They once soared over most of the western United States, but by 1982 there were fewer than 25 of these birds. California condors bred in captivity are now being released into the wild.

Jay

Blue jays are smart birds with loud, often harsh calls. They dine on nuts, berries, insects, and sometimes, other birds' eggs.

Bluebird

People help eastern bluebirds by building and maintaining nesting boxes. Bluebirds also nest in tree holes made by woodpeckers.

Blackbird

Male red-winged blackbirds show off their red wing patches and sing loudly to claim their wetland territories. The brown-striped females, perfectly camouflaged, can hide on the nest low in the cattails or reeds.

Bobwhite

Northern bobwhite is a species of quail named for its call, "bob-white!" Bobwhite usually hide in grasses and are hard to find by sight. At night a covey of quail forms a circle, with heads facing outward, on alert for danger.

Brant

Brant are geese that nest in the far north, on the Canadian and Alaskan tundra.

Oystercatcher

When an oyster has its shell a little bit open, an American oystercatcher can poke its red bill inside and cut the muscles that hold the shell closed. Then it can easily open the shell and dine.

Ovenbird

Ovenbirds walk the forest floor, searching leaves and fallen logs for insects to eat. Their call sounds like "teacher, teacher, teacher."

Cormorant

Double-crested cormorants are expert divers and fish finders. They often rest on branches and spread their wings to dry.

House Wren

House wrens build nests in tree hollows, birdhouses, and even mailboxes. The male builds several nests and then takes the female on a tour. She chooses a nest, finishes it, and lays eggs.

Hummingbird

Ruby-throated hummingbirds drink flower nectar, sip sap from trees, and hunt insects. These tiny birds weigh less than a penny.

White-winged Dove

This southwestern dove has white crescents on its wings. You may hear its long cooing call in desert and scrublands.

APRIL PULLEY SAYRE has rescued baby barn owls, fed baby woodpeckers, and been pecked on the head by an Arctic tern. She is an award-winning author of more than 50 books for young readers, including *Trout, Trout, Trout! (A Fish Chant)* and *Ant, Ant, Ant! (An Insect Chant)*. April and her husband, Jeff, a native plants expert, have turned their Indiana backyard into a paradise for birds. Between school visits and conference appearances, they travel to birding hotspots such as Panama. For curriculum links, see www.aprilsayre.com.

In his country studio in the Missouri Ozarks, GARY LOCKE draws pictures of birds and cows and various other things. He understands that birds do not really have big, beautiful teeth, but if they did, he thinks they would smile more, and brush with very tiny toothbrushes. For fun (since drawing birds with teeth counts as work) Gary likes to play football and race in triathlons. He lives with his one wife, one son, two daughters, one dog, one ferret, and an ever-changing number of cats. This is Gary's second picture book for children.